Birthday Hiccups

by Violet Findley
illustrated by Mary Sullivan

SCHOLASTIC INC.

New York • Toronto • London • Auckland
Sydney • Mexico City • New Delhi • Hong Kong

ISBN 978-0-545-68608-2

Copyright © 2010 by Lefty's Editorial Services.

All rights reserved. Published by Scholastic Inc.

SCHOLASTIC, LET'S LEARN READERS™, and associated logos
are trademarks and/or registered trademarks of Scholastic Inc.

12 11 10 9 8 7 6 5 4 3 2 1   14 15 16 17 18 19/0

Printed in China.

Hooray! It was Henry's birthday and he could not wait to celebrate. But then Henry got a surprise…

PREDICT

What do you think Henry's surprise might be?

Uh-oh, Henry had the hiccups.

QUESTION ? Do you think Henry likes this surprise? Why or why not?

Henry went to find his mother. She would know how to cure hiccups.

"Drink this big glass of water," she said.

Henry drank the water, but it did not work.

Henry went to find his father. He would know how to cure hiccups.

"Stand on your head," he said.

CONNECT

Have you ever had the hiccups? How did you try to cure them?

7

Henry stood on his head, but it did not work.

Henry went to find his sister. She would know how to cure hiccups.

"Hold your breath and hop on one foot," she said.

What is Henry's sister hiding under her pillow? Why?

9

Henry held his breath and hopped on one foot, but it did not work.

Henry went to find his grandma. She would know how to cure hiccups.

"Sit on the front steps," she said. "Then put your hands on top of your head and sing a silly song for 20 minutes."

QUESTION

Do you think this cure will work? Why or why not?

Henry sat on the front steps. He put his hands on top of his head and sang a silly song for 20 minutes. But that didn't work either.

Henry was getting upset. This was no way to spend his birthday! He opened the door and went back inside.

 VISUALIZE

Close your eyes. What do you see happening when Henry goes inside?

"SURPRISE!" shouted his family. "Happy Birthday!"

Henry was so shocked he jumped high into the air.

Then Henry got another surprise: His hiccups were gone! His family had scared them away just in time for cake. *Yum! Yum! Yum!*

TIE UP

Who has the hiccups now?

Story Prompts

Answer these questions after you have read the book.

1 What are Henry's family members each doing to get ready for his birthday? Look back through the pictures and see.

2 Do you think this story could happen in real life? Why or why not?

3 On Henry's next birthday, he loses a tooth. What happens? Turn on your imagination and tell a story about it!